Asthma

by Judith Peacock

Consultant:
Catherine Dolan, MD
Riverside Family Physicians, Minneapolis

Perspectives on Disease and Illness

LifeMatters
an imprint of Capstone Press
Mankato, Minnesota

LifeMatters books are published by Capstone Press
818 North Willow Street • Mankato, Minnesota 56001
http://www.capstone-press.com

Printed in the United States of America

Library of Congress Cataloging-in-Publication Data
Peacock, Judith, 1942–
     Asthma / by Judith Peacock.
          p.   cm. — (Perspectives on disease and illness.)
     Includes bibliographical references and index.
     Summary: Describes the causes, symptoms, diagnosis, complications, and treatment of various types of asthma.
     ISBN 07368-0283-5 (book). — ISBN 0-7368-0294-0 (series)
     1. Asthma Juvenile literature. [1. Asthma. 2. Diseases.]
     I. Title. II. Series.
     RC591.P42 2000
     616.2´38—dc21   99-30564
                                          CIP

Staff Credits
Kristin Thoennes, Rebecca Aldridge, editors; Adam Lazar, designer; Kimberly Danger, photo researcher

Photo Credits
Cover: The Stock Market/©Howard Sochurek, bottom; PNI/©Digital Vision, left, right; PNI/©Rubberball, middle
Index Stock Photography, Inc./20, 50
International Stock/©Dario Perla, 9
Photo Network/7, 44; ©Esbin-Anderson, 17
Photri-Microstock/41; ©Tom McCarthy, 11, 25, 31
Unicorn Stock Photos/©Fred Reischl, 14; ©Herbert L. Stormont, 32; ©Martin R. Jones, 37; ©Martha McBride, 38; ©Tom McCarthy, 55; ©Deneve Bunde, 46; ©Aneal Vohra, 59
Uniphoto Picture Agency/©Kit Kittle, 28
Visuals Unlimited/©Mark E. Gibson, 57

A 0 9 8 7 6 5 4 3 2 1

Table of Contents

8-02 Rainbow

Chapter Overview

Asthma is a chronic inflammation of the airways. People with asthma have episodes in which breathing becomes difficult.

During an asthma attack, the lining of the airways becomes swollen. Muscles surrounding the airways tighten. As a result, the inside of the airways becomes narrower. The airways also may become blocked with mucus. Air can no longer move freely in and out of the lungs.

Something must happen to cause an asthma attack. This something is called an asthma trigger. Common asthma triggers include allergens, air pollution, respiratory infections, weather extremes, emotional stress, and exercise.

Asthma is a serious condition. It affects millions of people worldwide. In the United States, it is the number one chronic disease of children age 18 and younger.

Chapter 1

What Is Asthma?

It was Saturday afternoon and time for Goldie's bath. Jed and his brother, Ben,

Jed, Age 13

lathered up the big golden retriever. Then they began to rinse her off. Suddenly, Jed felt his chest tightening up. He began to cough. He tried taking gulps of air. It was harder and harder to breathe. Jed gave Ben a scared look. "Get Mom and Dad!" he gasped.

The boys' parents came running. By this time, Jed's lips were turning blue. His parents gathered him up and put him in the car. Ben jumped in the backseat beside his brother. The frantic family headed for the emergency room. They left Goldie wringing wet in the bathtub.

Of people who have asthma, children between ages 11 and 18 have the most problems with the illness.

Jed had an asthma attack. Asthma is a disorder of the lungs. Unlike other lung diseases, asthma is episodic. That means asthma attacks come and go. During an attack, people with asthma have difficulty breathing. An attack may last for several minutes or for days. Attacks range from slight breathlessness to not being able to breathe at all.

Asthma can be chronic. That means a person can have the illness for a long time. It may even last a lifetime. About 15 million people in the United States have asthma. One-third of them are children under the age of 18. Nearly two million people in Canada have asthma. One-third of them are children as well. Asthma is the number one chronic disease of children and teens.

A Lung Disorder

The lungs are part of the respiratory system. Inhaling, or breathing in, brings oxygen to the bloodstream. Exhaling, or breathing out, releases a waste gas from the blood. This gas is called carbon dioxide. During an attack, people with asthma have difficulty exhaling. Stale air fills and becomes trapped in the lungs. It becomes harder to inhale enough fresh air.

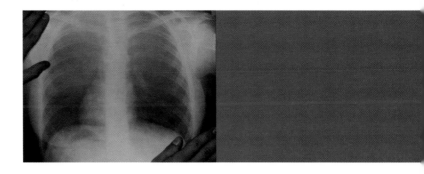

Normally, air enters the body through the nose or mouth. It travels through the larynx (voice box) and enters the trachea (windpipe). The windpipe divides into two main branches. These branches are called bronchial tubes. One branch goes into the left lung. The other goes into the right lung. In the lungs, the bronchial tubes divide into smaller tubes, or bronchioles. They deliver oxygen throughout the lungs. A thin layer of mucus coats the inner walls of the airways and helps to cleanse the air.

During an asthma attack, several things happen. The muscles surrounding the air tubes tighten. This is called a bronchospasm. The lining of the air tubes becomes inflamed. When something is inflamed that means it may be red, hot, or swollen. These two events narrow the opening of the airways. In addition, mucus production increases. This sticky liquid plugs up airways. All this slows or stops the flow of air in and out of the lungs. Breathing becomes difficult.

Asthma Triggers

People with asthma have chronically inflamed airways. Their airways are very sensitive to things that do not bother other people. Experts are not sure what causes this inflammation. Between attacks, most people with asthma breathe normally. Then something happens to cause an attack. This something is called an asthma trigger. Asthma triggers vary from person to person. There are hundreds of possible triggers.

The word *asthma* comes from a Greek word meaning "to pant."

Allergens

In some people, the body's immune, or defense, system overreacts to allergens. Common allergens include pollen, mold, feathers, and animal saliva and dander. Dander are tiny flakes of skin. The droppings of cockroaches and house dust mites may cause many people to wheeze and sneeze. People also can be allergic to certain foods such as milk, eggs, nuts, and fish. All of these allergic reactions can trigger asthma attacks.

Asthma and allergies often go together. A person can have allergies and not have asthma. Likewise, a person can have asthma and not have allergies. However, at least 80 percent of children and 50 percent of adults with asthma also have allergies.

Outdoor Air Pollution

Smog, soot, and sulfur dioxide can irritate the lungs. These irritants result from burning fuel in factories and power plants. Automobile exhaust also releases pollutants into the air.

Indoor Air Pollution

Smoke from fireplaces and stoves can cause asthma attacks. Smoking cigarettes is one of the worst triggers. Secondhand smoke, or smoke from other people's cigarettes, also is a common trigger.

Chemical fumes from household cleaners, paints, and other products can be asthma triggers. Even hair spray and perfume can be dangerous for some people with asthma.

Gwen has joined the campaign for a scent-free America. She wants laws that ban **Gwen, Age 17** perfume in public places. Gwen used to think such laws were silly. Then she discovered that perfume is one of her asthma triggers. Gwen no longer wears perfume herself. But other people's fragrances bother her. At the movies, she often must move to a different seat. She cannot walk by the cosmetic counter in a department store without gasping. The most embarrassing situation of all involves dating. Gwen must ask her boyfriends not to wear aftershave lotion or cologne.

Infections of the Respiratory System
Illnesses such as a cold, the flu, or a sore throat can produce an episode of asthma. Respiratory infections are the most common trigger in young children with asthma.

Myth: A hot, dry climate is best for people with asthma.

Fact: A hot, dry climate may help people whose asthma is triggered by cold weather. However, no geographic location is safe from asthma triggers. People with asthma usually become sensitive to triggers in the new location. Asthma can be controlled in almost any environment. Only in rare cases should people move because of their asthma.

Weather

Various weather conditions can set off asthma attacks. Windy days scatter more allergens in the air. A light rainfall increases the buildup of mold. Cold weather causes people to breathe in through their mouth instead of their nose. The air does not get warmed up before reaching the lungs. Cool air can touch off an attack in people with sensitive airways.

Emotional Stress and Excitement

At one time it was thought that people with asthma were emotionally ill. Doctors thought asthma was a response to emotional problems. Now doctors know that emotions do not cause the condition. However, any emotion that involves deep, rapid breathing can trigger an attack. This includes crying, anger, frustration, yelling, and even laughter.

Vigorous Exercise

Long-distance or nonstop exercising can irritate the airways. Cross-country running, treadmill running, and bicycle racing are especially hard on a person's breathing. Cold-weather events such as ice hockey and cross-country skiing can double the irritation.

Who Gets Asthma?

Asthma tends to run in families. Some people inherit a tendency to get asthma. Then they need something to trigger it.

Asthma affects all races and all ages. In children, asthma is most likely to occur before age five. Young children are especially open to attack because their lungs are still developing. Among adults, asthma usually appears for the first time between the ages of 30 and 39. About 10 percent of new cases occur in people age 65 and older.

Childhood asthma affects boys more than girls. Around the age of 12, however, the situation reverses. Girls with asthma begin to outnumber boys with asthma. The beginning of a girl's menstrual periods may explain the reversal. Some doctors think that hormones may be another asthma trigger.

Asthma is not contagious. It cannot be passed from person to person like a cold or the flu.

Points to Consider

What did you know about asthma before reading this chapter?

Do you know anyone who has asthma? What is asthma like for them?

Have you ever been in a situation where you couldn't get enough air? What did it feel like?

Chapter Overview

Asthma can be classified by severity, or how often asthma attacks occur. There are four levels: severe persistent asthma, moderate persistent asthma, mild persistent asthma, and mild intermittent asthma.

Asthma also can be classified by the substance or situation that triggers an attack. For example, a person might have exercise-induced asthma, allergy-related asthma, infectious asthma, or occupational asthma.

Most children with moderate to severe asthma will continue to have asthma as adults. Their symptoms may ease in adulthood, however.

Chapter 2

Types of Asthma

There are different ways of classifying asthma. That means asthma is separated into groups according to certain characteristics. One way is according to the severity of attacks. Another way is according to the source, or trigger, for the attack.

Severity of Attack

The National Asthma Education and Prevention Program classifies asthma according to its severity. Severity refers to how often a person has asthma attacks. People with asthma have different levels of severity.

The Four Levels of Severity

Severe Persistent Asthma	Adam has severe persistent asthma. This is the most dangerous type. Adam's symptoms, or evidence of illness, occur frequently. He coughs almost constantly. His chest feels congested all the time. Adam has frequent, serious attacks. His asthma has landed him in the hospital many times.
Moderate Persistent Asthma	Maureen's asthma is the moderate persistent type. She has one or more symptoms each day. She has a full-blown asthma attack at least twice a week. Maureen sometimes must go to the emergency room for treatment.
Mild Persistent Asthma	Keith has mild persistent asthma. Keith notices breathing problems several times a week. He never has symptoms more than once a day.
Mild Intermittent Asthma	Kayla has mild intermittent asthma. She has symptoms two or fewer times a week. Kayla can go for weeks or months without an asthma attack.

Any person with asthma can die as a result of an asthma attack. However, asthma is usually less life threatening to people with milder forms.

Do you wonder what an asthma attack is like?
Listen to what these teens with asthma say.

"It's like being trapped underwater. You're scared you're going to drown."—Helen, age 16

"It's like having an elephant sit on your chest."—Quentin, age 13

"I feel like I'm suffocating."—Yvette, age 14

"You feel like someone has knocked the wind out of you."—Bryant, age 15

Source of Attack

Asthma also is classified by the substance or situation that triggers an attack. For example, some people with asthma have their attacks following vigorous exercise. This type of asthma is called exercise-induced asthma, or EIA. People whose asthma is triggered by allergies are said to have allergy-related asthma. Infectious asthma is asthma triggered by colds and other respiratory infections. A person whose attacks come mainly at night has nocturnal asthma.

Ruthie, Age 15

Ruthie's dad was a housepainter. Several months ago, Mr. Larson began having asthma attacks. He realized that his attacks came only while he was at work. Mr. Larson's doctor sent him to an allergy specialist. The allergist said that Mr. Larson is allergic to chemicals in housepaint. He has occupational asthma. Mr. Larson had to find another job. He could not breathe and paint houses at the same time.

You can get an idea of what an asthma attack is like. Hold your nostrils shut. Then try breathing through a straw.

Outgrowing Childhood Asthma

Do children and teens outgrow their asthma? At one time, this was believed to be the case. New research sheds more light on this matter. According to the American Lung Association, 75 percent of children with moderate to severe asthma retain their asthma as adults.

Adults may think their asthma has gone away. As children grow, their airways grow larger. This helps to ease symptoms. In addition, the lifestyle of adults changes. They do not spend as much time outdoors. They may not encounter asthma triggers such as pollen as often. Adults who believe they have outgrown their asthma might stop treating their condition. This can be dangerous. Airways might become permanently scarred and blocked.

Points to Consider

Have you ever had breathing problems because of a bad chest cold, bronchitis, or pneumonia? What did it feel like? What did you do to help yourself breathe better?

How might having asthma affect a teen's life?

Which level of asthma severity is the most serious? Why?

Chapter Overview

Early diagnosis of asthma is important. Asthma can be difficult to diagnose. It resembles other respiratory diseases.

The main symptoms of asthma are coughing, gasping for air, tightness in the chest, and mucus in the throat. These symptoms may be ongoing, or they may appear suddenly.

Doctors diagnose asthma on the basis of the person's symptoms, medical history, physical examination, and laboratory tests. Pulmonary-function tests are the most important tests in diagnosing asthma.

Chapter 3

Diagnosing Asthma

Early diagnosis, or determination, of asthma is important. If left untreated, asthma can lead to permanent lung damage. It even may be life threatening.

Diagnosing asthma can be difficult. Its symptoms are similar to those of other respiratory diseases. When a person with undiagnosed asthma goes to the doctor, he or she usually feels fine. The doctor may need to provoke, or start, an attack. Witnessing an attack helps the doctor tell if the person has asthma.

Asthma Symptoms

This is LaTarsha's third year on her high school's track team. Her events are the 200 meter and the 400 meter. She is one of the best runners in the conference. LaTarsha hopes to get a track scholarship to college.

LaTarsha, Age 17

LaTarsha's coach is worried about her. In the locker room after practice, LaTarsha coughs and wheezes. She does the same on the bus after track meets. The coach thinks LaTarsha might have asthma. She suggested that LaTarsha see a doctor.

LaTarsha has symptoms of asthma. She coughs a lot after exercising. She makes a wheezing, or whistling, sound when she breathes.

Thousands of people have "hidden" asthma.
They have few or no outward symptoms. They
may never go to the doctor for diagnosis. Their
only clue might be frequent respiratory illness or
a persistent cough.

Other physical symptoms of asthma include the following:

Difficulty breathing (more than just shortness of breath)

Tightness in the chest

A lot of mucus in the throat

Coughing attacks after laughing or crying

Coughing attacks during the night

A person with asthma may have one or more of these symptoms.
Asthma symptoms vary from person to person. Symptoms may
appear suddenly, or they may occur regularly.

There are other signs of asthma as well. People with asthma may
be irritable because of the discomfort. They may dislike playing
sports because they get winded too easily. They may avoid going
places where they must climb many stairs or walk long distances.

Steps in Diagnosis

Laboratory tests are an important part of diagnosing asthma.
Pulmonary-function tests are the most important. These tests
measure how well the lungs are working. They also tell how well
the lungs respond to treatment.

LaTarsha took her coach's advice. She went to see her family doctor.

LaTarsha's Exam

LaTarsha's doctor thought she might have asthma. He wanted to be sure. He sent LaTarsha to a pulmonary internist. A pulmonary internist is a doctor who specializes in lung disorders.

The specialist first took LaTarsha's medical history. He wanted to know if anyone in LaTarsha's family had asthma. He found out that LaTarsha had many colds and respiratory infections as a child. She is allergic to milk and eggs. Next came a physical examination. The doctor listened to LaTarsha's breathing. He checked her breathing muscles. He also examined her eyes, ears, nose, and throat for signs of infection.

The doctor showed LaTarsha a device called a spirometer. He told her to blow into the breathing tube. LaTarsha blew out as hard and as fast as she could. The exhaled air pushed the needle on the scale into the normal zone.

Then the doctor wanted to test LaTarsha's breathing during an asthma attack. He had her run on a treadmill for eight minutes. LaTarsha's symptoms soon appeared. She began coughing and wheezing. Then she breathed into the spirometer. This time the needle barely rose on the scale.

The doctor gave LaTarsha medicine to stop the coughing and wheezing. LaTarsha breathed into the spirometer once again. The needle jumped higher than the last time.

Other tests doctors might use in diagnosing asthma include:

Chest X rays. Chest X rays do not reveal asthma. Instead, they help the doctor rule out other diseases such as cystic fibrosis, pneumonia, or heart disease.

Allergy skin testing. The doctor orders allergy skin testing if allergies seem to cause the person's asthma attacks. Allergy skin testing identifies the specific allergens that trigger the attack.

Blood tests. Blood tests can indicate the presence of other diseases. Having another disease might complicate asthma treatment.

Sputum tests. Sputum is liquid coughed up from the lungs. Studying a sample of sputum might show substances related to asthma.

Chinese manuscripts from 5,000 years ago describe asthma and its treatment. The Chinese used the bark of ephedra trees to produce ephedrine. This is the first-known drug for the treatment of any allergic disease.

After the Diagnosis

LaTarsha's Diagnosis

The specialist confirmed that LaTarsha has asthma. The pulmonary-function test settled the diagnosis. Asthma is a reversible disease of the airways. This means that the blocked air tubes can be opened. LaTarsha's airways were blocked during the second spirometer test. Then she took medicine to relieve her symptoms. Her performance improved on the third spirometer test.

LaTarsha's asthma is exercise induced. Exercise-induced asthma is one of the most treatable forms. LaTarsha will still be able to participate in track. LaTarsha's coach said she would help LaTarsha manage her asthma. The coach knows all about the disease. She has asthma, too.

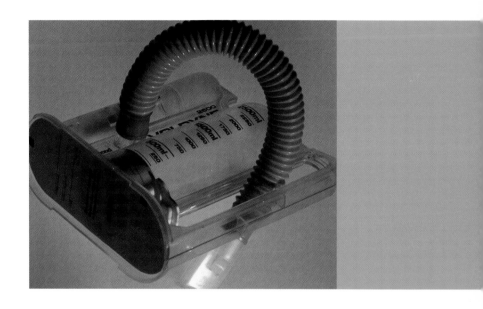

Points to Consider

Describe a time you were sick and didn't know what you had. What were your symptoms? What steps did the doctor take to diagnose your illness?

Do you know anyone who has symptoms of asthma? How would you convince that person to see a doctor?

How would you react if you found out you had asthma?

Chapter Overview

Asthma cannot be cured, but it can be controlled. With proper treatment, people with asthma can be as active as they want to be.

Avoiding asthma triggers is the most basic way to control asthma.

Asthma medications are very helpful in controlling asthma. There are two main kinds: relievers and controllers. Bronchodilators relieve symptoms on a short-term basis. Anti-inflammatories help to control symptoms over the long term. Some people with asthma need both kinds of medications.

People with asthma can use a peak flow meter to check their breathing. A low score indicates that air tubes are becoming blocked.

Exercise and relaxation techniques can be part of a program to control asthma.

Chapter 4

Controlling Asthma

There is no cure for asthma. It can be controlled with proper treatment. Control means that asthma does not interfere with a healthy, normal life. People with asthma can achieve this by following their treatment program.

Avoiding Asthma Triggers

The most obvious way to control asthma is to figure out the cause of attacks. Then, if possible, the person can stay away from the trigger. The person might be able to remove it from his or her surroundings. By avoiding their triggers, people with asthma may have fewer attacks. Their attacks may be less severe.

People with asthma might discover their triggers through trial and error. In allergy-related cases, allergy testing may reveal the source. Allergy shots will help the person tolerate the allergen. He or she must still continue to avoid the allergen when possible.

Tiara's five-year-old brother, Juwan, has asthma. Juwan's allergist says that dust mites cause the little boy's asthma attacks. Once or twice a week, Tiara and her mother vacuum and dust the house. Their vacuum has a special filter and a double bag to trap the dust. Tiara wet-mops all the uncarpeted floors. Her mother strips Juwan's bed and washes the bedding in hot water. Dust mites thrive in sheets, pillowcases, and bedspreads. During all this cleaning, Juwan must wear a face mask or leave the house. He doesn't want to breathe in the dust that his mother and sister stir up.

Tiara, Age 18

Children and teens with asthma are likely to encounter asthma triggers at school. Their families should ask for the school's cooperation in removing these triggers or helping students avoid them. In some cases, activities may need to be modified. For example, on windy or cold days students with asthma may need to stay indoors for gym class.

Medications

Medications play an important part in controlling asthma. There are two main classes of medications for asthma. One class is bronchodilators. Bronchodilators provide quick relief during an asthma attack. They relax bronchial muscles. The air tubes open up, and the person can breathe again.

The other class of medications is anti-inflammatories. Anti-inflammatories provide ongoing control of asthma. They reduce swelling in the air tubes and make the tubes less sensitive to triggers.

For best results, drug therapy for people with moderate to severe asthma must include both bronchodilators and anti-inflammatories. Anti-inflammatories help to reduce the number and severity of asthma attacks. They help to prevent permanent damage to the airways. Some people with mild asthma use only bronchodilators. They take medicine only when they are coughing and wheezing.

Some people with asthma may take over-the-counter asthma drugs to relieve their symptoms. These drugs contain a mixture of ingredients. Some may be good for a person. Others may be bad. It is best to work with a doctor. Asthma symptoms and triggers can change. A doctor can prescribe a medicine and dosage that fit the person's symptoms. People with asthma should always take medication exactly as prescribed. They should let their doctors know if the medicine is not helping.

In the United States, it costs over $3 billion a year to treat asthma in children under age 18. This includes the cost of medication, doctors, emergency room visits, and hospital stays.

Taking Asthma Medications

Asthma medications are generally inhaled. Inhaling increases the effectiveness of the medicine. It also helps reduce side effects. Some asthma medications may be swallowed or injected.

Most people with asthma use an inhaler for their medication. An inhaler is a handheld device. It can fit into a pocket or a purse. A canister of liquid asthma medicine goes inside the inhaler. The person holds the inhaler upright and inserts the mouthpiece into his or her mouth. Many children and some adults use a 4- to 8-inch tube between the mouthpiece and mouth. This "spacer" helps distribute the medicine evenly in the bronchial tubes. When the person presses on the inhaler, it delivers a dose of medicine as a spray. The person inhales the medicine directly into the lungs. Metered-dose inhalers release a set amount of medicine.

Inhalers can be tricky to use. Small children or others who have difficulty with an inhaler might use a nebulizer instead. A nebulizer turns liquid asthma medicine into a mist. The person breathes in the mist for about 15 or 20 minutes. Nebulizers are not portable like metered-dose inhalers, but the mist goes deeper into the lungs.

Taking Asthma Medications at School

Children and teens with asthma may need to take medication during the school day. School personnel should know the child's medication plan. They should know whether the child needs help taking the medication. Some schools do not allow students to carry medication with them. All prescription medicines must be kept in the nurse's office. Other schools allow students to carry medicine but specify where students can take it. For example, a student may need to step into the hall to use his or her inhaler.

Monitoring Air Flow

Peak flow meters are another way to control asthma. A peak flow meter is a portable measuring device. It measures the amount of air exhaled from the lungs. The person with asthma blows as hard as possible into a tube. A needle on the device indicates the person's score. The person does this three times. Then he or she takes the highest score and compares it to a standard score. The standard score is the amount of air a healthy person of the same sex, age, and height can exhale.

The peak flow meter is like a thermometer or blood pressure cuff. It can warn of health problems. A score below the standard score might indicate that the person's airways are closing. An asthma attack might be on its way. Then the person can adjust his or her medication to head off the attack. If the person's score is in the danger zone, he or she should contact a doctor immediately.

Theo is in junior high. He was recently diagnosed with asthma. His doctor put him on a medication schedule. She taught him how to use an inhaler and a peak flow monitor. It is all very complicated. Theo, however, is slowly getting better. Before treatment began, he had two or three attacks a day. Now he hardly has two a week. Best of all, he and his parents have peace of mind. They don't have to worry that each breath could be Theo's last.

Theo, Age 13

Exercise

Exercise can be a big part of an asthma treatment program. Many champion athletes entered sports as a way of controlling their asthma. Exercise can greatly improve lung capacity. An exercise program should be well planned and supervised. People with asthma should take asthma medication before and after exercising. They should bring their inhalers along. Warming up gradually is important, too.

Some sports are better than others for people with asthma. Sports that require constant motion such as soccer and cross-country running should be avoided. They are too stressful on the lungs. Sports such as baseball and volleyball that require short bursts of energy are better. Swimming in an indoor, heated pool benefits many people with asthma. The warm, moist air is good for their lungs. The swimmer's horizontal position helps to loosen mucus.

Many athletes have excelled in sports despite having asthma. Here are just two:

Jackie Joyner-Kersee, 1988 and 1992 Olympic gold medallist in track

Tom Dolan, 1996 Olympic gold medallist in swimming

Alternative Treatments

Natural remedies may help to control asthma as well. Breathing exercises and meditation promote slower, deeper breathing. These techniques can relax the lungs and improve asthma symptoms. Some people believe that certain foods protect against asthma. People with asthma should eat a balanced diet for the sake of good health. There is no strong proof, however, that nutrition affects asthma.

Points to Consider

What things in your school's environment might trigger an asthma attack?

Why might schools not allow students to carry prescription medications? What is your school's policy on prescription medications? How could you find out?

Why might it be hard for a teen with asthma to stick to a treatment program?

How could you help a friend with asthma follow his or her treatment program?

Chapter Overview

People with asthma should be prepared for an asthma attack. They should know their asthma warning signals and discuss an emergency action plan with their doctors. They should have a supply of medication on hand.

People with asthma should inform family, friends, and co-workers about their condition. These people may need to assist the person with asthma during an asthma attack.

Smoking, drinking alcohol, and doing other drugs can bring on an asthma attack. They also can make recovery from an attack more difficult.

Chapter 5

What to Do During an Asthma Attack

Even with proper treatment, a person still may have an asthma attack. An asthma attack can be frightening. It is frightening not only for the person having the attack but also for anybody watching. Knowing what to do can help ease people's fears and even save lives.

Fast Fact

Children and teens with asthma make many trips to hospital emergency rooms. In the United States, asthma accounts for one in six of all pediatric emergency visits.

Early Warning Signs

Certain signals generally appear before an asthma attack. They warn the person that an attack is coming. The signals can be seen, heard, and felt. Some examples of signals include the following:

Runny nose

Sleeplessness, restlessness

Slight changes in breathing

Coughing and sneezing not caused by a cold

Every person with asthma has his or her own pattern of signals. People with asthma can learn to identify their signals. They should discuss with their doctor what to do when these signals occur. Adult caregivers need to be alert to warning signals in young children with asthma.

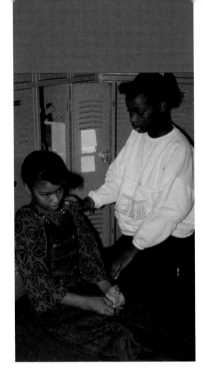

Moderate or Mild Asthma Attacks

Fran and Olivia raced up the stairs. They had one minute to make it to class. If they arrived after the bell, they would have to spend the hour in detention. Then they would miss an important test. At the top of the steps, Fran began wheezing and coughing.

Fran, Age 16

"I can't breathe," she panted. "You go ahead."

"Is it your asthma?" Olivia asked. Fran nodded. There was a look of panic in her eyes. Olivia searched her friend's purse. She found Fran's inhaler and gave it to her.

"Here," she said calmly. "Take it easy. You're going to be all right. I'll stay with you." Fran inhaled her medication. After a few minutes, she began breathing easier. Olivia walked with Fran to the nurse's office. After checking Fran's breathing, the nurse gave the girls a pass to get into class.

Fran had a mild to moderate asthma attack. People with asthma can treat this level of attack themselves. They can use their bronchodilators. These devices usually provide relief within 5 to 10 minutes. If breathing does not become easier within a specified time, a doctor should be notified. If possible, the asthma trigger should be removed.

Even a mild to moderate asthma attack can be dangerous. Fortunately, Fran had told Olivia about her asthma. Olivia knew how to help her friend. She did something very important. Olivia remained calm and confident. This helped Fran relax, too. During an attack, the person with asthma may panic. This increases the need for air and makes breathing more difficult.

Myth: During an asthma attack, a person should drink lots of liquid.

Fact: Liquids will not help a person get over an asthma attack any quicker. He or she should drink only a reasonable amount.

Severe Asthma Attacks

Shawn's mother has asthma. One Friday night, Shawn went to the movies with his friends. When he arrived home, he found his mother sitting at the kitchen table. She was slumped forward with her shoulders raised. Her nostrils were flared, and she was breathing rapidly. Her lips and fingernails were turning blue-gray. When she saw Shawn, she tried to talk. He could barely hear her. Shawn knew what to do. This had happened before. He called 911.

Shawn, Age 17

Shawn's mother had a severe asthma attack. She needed emergency medical treatment. People having a severe asthma attack may be hospitalized. They may need to have mucus suctioned from their lungs. They may need to be put on a respirator, or breathing machine. The respirator increases the level of oxygen in the blood and decreases the level of carbon dioxide.

Some people have a severe allergic reaction to certain foods or to a bee sting. They may not have time to go to the emergency room. Their throat begins closing up almost immediately. These people should carry an Epi Pen. The person presses the Epi Pen against his or her thigh. It releases a dose of adrenaline to open the airways.

An Asthma Attack in School

Teens and children with asthma may have an attack during the school day. Parents need to prepare school personnel for dealing with an attack. The principal, school nurse, and teachers should have a written rescue plan. Such a plan contains the following information:

Symptoms of teen's asthma attacks

Teen's personal best peak flow reading

Steps to take during an asthma attack

When to seek emergency care

Person or persons to contact in an emergency

Emergency asthma medications

Tobacco, Alcohol, and Other Drugs

Tobacco, alcohol, and other drugs can be dangerous for anyone. They are especially dangerous for people with asthma. First, those drugs can make asthma worse. They also can trigger an attack. Second, tobacco, alcohol, and other drugs can alter the speed at which asthma medications work.

Points to Consider

Why might children and teens with asthma have a high number of emergency room visits?

Whom should teens with asthma tell about their condition?

What could you do to help a person during an asthma attack?

Why should people with asthma avoid tobacco, alcohol, and other drugs?

Chapter Overview

Living with asthma can be hard for anyone. It presents special challenges to teens.

Asthma can interfere with a teen's desire to fit in. It can strain relationships with family and friends. It can affect success in school.

There are ways for teens with asthma to cope with their disease. The most important way is to follow the treatment plan. When asthma is under control, most asthma-related problems disappear.

Dealing with asthma can have a positive side. Teens can learn about self-discipline. They can build a stronger body.

Chapter 6

Living With Asthma

Living with a chronic illness like asthma can be difficult. It is especially difficult for teenagers. Teens are already dealing with the hard task of growing up. Dealing with asthma along with everything else can be overwhelming. In addition, physical changes during adolescence may make a teen's asthma harder to control.

Fitting In

Most teens want to be like everyone else their age. They fear being different. Asthma makes teens different. Teens with asthma take medicine and use inhalers. They must be on the lookout constantly for asthma triggers. Some teens try to deny their asthma. This usually makes things worse.

In the United States, teens and children with asthma miss 10 million school days each year. Asthma is the number one chronic condition causing children to be absent from school.

Wyatt, Age 15

Wyatt was a new kid in school. He was trying hard to make friends. No one knew about his asthma. "If they find out, they'll think I'm a wimp," Wyatt reasoned. "This is my chance to start over."

One Saturday, some boys in Wyatt's homeroom invited him to go bowling. Wyatt knew the bowling alley would probably be smoky, but he didn't care. He was just glad to be included.

After about a half hour, Wyatt could feel his chest tightening up. He tried to pretend it wasn't happening. By the fifth frame, he was coughing and wheezing. Wyatt prayed for the end of the game. He wanted to go into the men's room and use his inhaler. "If I pull it out here," Wyatt reasoned, "they'll think I'm some sort of weirdo."

Wyatt struggled to throw the ball down the alley. He could only manage gutter balls. The other boys rolled their eyes and shook their heads. Wyatt's turn came in the eighth frame. As he tried to lift the ball from the ball return, he lost his balance and fell backward. Wyatt lay sprawled out on the floor, gasping for air. One of the boys got the bowling alley manager. She called for the paramedics. By Monday morning, everyone in school knew what had happened.

Missing School

Teens with asthma may miss a lot of school. They may feel tired after an episode. They may need to go to the doctor frequently. As a result, it can be difficult to keep up with schoolwork.

Teens with asthma should explain their situation to teachers and other school personnel. Teachers may allow more time for assignments. Tutoring or homebound teaching may be available. Teens with asthma should find someone in each class to take notes and carry home assignments. Special arrangements such as these can keep the teen from falling behind.

Telling Others

Teens with asthma may wonder what to tell others about their condition. They certainly should tell their close friends. Knowing about asthma will keep friends from getting scared if they see an attack. They even may be able to help.

Telling friends and others about asthma triggers can help to avoid awkward situations. For example, a teen with asthma might be invited to a friend's house for dinner. If the teen has food allergies, he or she should mention this to the friend ahead of time. Then the family won't prepare food the teen can't eat.

Becoming Independent

Lynda was diagnosed with asthma when she was two years old. Her parents spent **Lynda, Age 13** many sleepless nights listening for her next breath. Lynda is a teenager now. She has her asthma under control, but her parents still worry. Every time she leaves the house, her parents say, "Do you have your inhaler with you?" If she sneezes or coughs, her parents are right there. "Are you okay?" they ask. Lynda wishes her parents would back off.

Overprotective parents are a problem for many teens with a chronic illness. Like other teens, they want to grow up and do things on their own. Their parents may be afraid to let them go. They worry how the teen will manage without them.

Teens with asthma deal with this problem in different ways. One teen got her mother to join a support group. Now her mother discusses her worries with other mothers of children with asthma. Another teen showed his parents that he could be trusted to take his medicine. He showed them he could handle an asthma attack.

"Asthma teaches you to be resilient. You learn to stand up to anything."—Perry, age 17

"Some people think that just because you've got asthma, you're weak. I always feel I have to prove myself."—Hassen, age 14

"If it hadn't been for asthma, I might not have gotten into sports. My doctor suggested swimming as a way to build my lung power."—Vonnie, age 16

"Don't be afraid to use your inhaler around friends. If they're really your friends, they'll understand."
—Terrell, age 13

"Having asthma has taught me that I can set a goal and achieve it. Kids with asthma can do anything they want!"—Juanita, age 15

Getting Along With Brothers and Sisters

Annette's asthma is triggered when she is around cats. She discovered this after being at her grandma's house for a week. While at Grandma's, she had no symptoms. The minute she got home, however, she started wheezing and sneezing. The big difference between Grandma's and home was her sister's new kittens. It occurred to Annette's parents that she might be allergic to cats. This proved to be the case. The family tried to keep the kittens away from Annette. It was no use. Their dander was all over the house. The family ended up giving the kittens away. Annette's sister was mad at Annette for the loss of the pets.

Annette, Age 14

Asthma affects a teen's brothers and sisters, too. They may have to give up things because of their sibling's asthma. Parents may show special attention to the child with asthma. Asthma attacks might put the home in constant turmoil. Brothers and sisters may come to resent the teen with asthma.

On the other hand, brothers and sisters might worry about their sibling. They might be scared he or she will die during an asthma attack. They might feel guilty about being healthy.

Maintaining a healthy home life can be challenging for families with children with asthma. Talking openly and honestly about problems and feelings will help. Counseling can help families overcome difficulties as well.

Making Adjustments

Certain activities and situations can trigger an asthma attack. Teens with asthma often must make adaptations in order to participate. This requires thinking ahead.

> Ron was excited. Camille had agreed to go to **Ron, Age 18** the prom with him. Then Ron realized something. His asthma is exercise induced. Dancing is a form of exercise. How could he keep from having an asthma attack at the prom? Ron made a plan. He would take asthma medication before hitting the dance floor. He would sit out every few dances. Ron hoped Camille would understand.

Coping With Asthma

Living with asthma can be challenging. Asthma, however, does not need to control a person's life. If you are a teen with asthma, here are ways you can cope:

Take your medicine.
Remember that you have asthma even when you're not having symptoms. Take your medicine as prescribed. Too little medicine may not help. Too much medicine can be harmful. Tell your doctor if you have troublesome side effects. He or she may be able to prescribe a different medication.

Be an active member of your health care team.
Keep track of when your episodes occur and how severe they are. Note what may have triggered the attack and the effectiveness of your medicine. Share this information with doctors, nurses, and others on your health care team. The information will help in planning your treatment program.

Discover your asthma triggers.
Be a detective. If you know your asthma triggers, stay away from them. Ask friends and family to help you.

Join a support group for teens with asthma.
You will learn how other teens manage their asthma. You can share problems and get advice. Asthma camps are another good place to meet teens who know what you're going through.

Learn all you can about asthma.
Knowledge is power. Many books, pamphlets, and videos are available. Some are especially for teens. A great deal of information is now available on the Internet.

Join an organization that works to improve life for people with asthma.
These organizations support asthma research and education. They work for laws to guarantee the rights of people with asthma. See the back of this book for a list of organizations.

Don't let asthma limit you.
Don't let it keep you from doing things you love to do. You can actively live your life.

Asthma-related deaths among teens have doubled in the last decade. Emergency room visits for this age group have risen as well. Experts believe that the desire of teens to fit in is the reason for this alarming trend. Many teenagers with asthma are not following their treatment program, because they do not want to be seen as different.

Points to Consider

What social situations might cause problems for a teen with asthma?

Your friends are making fun of a teen who is wheezing. What would you do?

If you had a friend with asthma, how would that affect your life?

Do you know anyone who has a chronic illness? How does the illness affect the person's life? How does the person cope?

Chapter Overview

The number of new asthma cases is rising. Asthma-related deaths also are increasing. This is happening despite advances in the treatment of asthma.

Several possible reasons account for the alarming rise in asthma cases. Some reasons involve failure to follow an asthma treatment program. Others involve increased asthma triggers in the environment.

There are ways to reverse the rise in asthma cases. Easier treatment methods might encourage people with asthma to stick to their programs. Improving air quality also would reduce the number of attacks.

Asthma education is important for everyone.

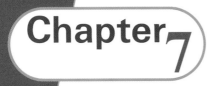

Chapter 7

Looking Ahead

Doctors and researchers know more about asthma than ever before. Treatments are more effective than at any time in the past. Instead of going down, however, the number of new cases of asthma is going up. In 1985, there were 8.5 million people with asthma in the United States. By 1995, this figure had jumped to 14.5 million. That number is even greater today.

Asthma-related deaths are on the rise, too. Asthma now kills about 5,500 Americans each year. This is double the number of deaths from 20 years ago.

Scientists someday may be able to identify an individual who is genetically at risk for asthma. They could then apply gene therapy to defective genes.

Asthma on the Rise

There are several possible reasons for the troubling increase in asthma. One reason may be people's failure to take asthma seriously. Some people deny their symptoms and refuse to seek treatment. Doctors themselves may treat asthma too lightly. Several medical authorities believe doctors should prescribe stronger medicine to control inflammation.

A second reason for the increase in asthma involves the difficulty of asthma treatment programs. Controlling asthma can be complicated and time-consuming. Some people with asthma follow their programs half-heartedly or simply give up.

Other possible explanations involve increased exposure to asthma triggers. Increased air pollution from factories and cars may be causing more asthma attacks. People spend more time in tightly constructed office buildings and homes. There is little exchange of natural air. As a result, people breathe in dust and chemical fumes that build up indoors.

Asthma among children and teens from poor city neighborhoods is rising. These young people often live in conditions that expose them to more asthma triggers. For example, crowded apartments put children at risk for respiratory infections. Housing that is not kept up attracts cockroaches. The children's asthma may get worse because their family cannot afford medical treatment.

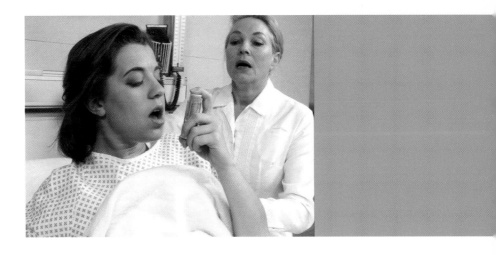

Easier Ways to Take Asthma Medications

Angie, a high school junior, hates taking her asthma medication. It's inconvenient and **Angie, Age 16** tastes terrible. It's embarrassing to have to use an inhaler. Besides, she has a hard time directing the spray correctly.

Recent studies reveal the following disturbing facts:

Only 12 to 14 percent of Americans with asthma regularly take anti-inflammatory drugs needed for prevention.

Seventy to eighty percent of people with asthma use their inhalers incorrectly. They do not get the full benefit of their medicine.

Twenty percent of people with asthma rarely or never carry inhalers with them.

In response to these findings, researchers are developing new drugs and devices for asthma medications. These will allow people with asthma more choices and methods. Easier ways to take asthma medications might help to reverse the rise in asthma cases.

Did You Know?

Metered-dose inhalers now have a new design. Inhalers use chlorofluorocarbons (CFCs) to propel medicine into the lungs. CFCs are thought to damage the Earth's ozone layer. The United States and other countries banned the manufacture of CFCs in 1996. Inhalers, however, received a temporary exemption. Drug companies now make CFC-free inhalers to comply with the ban.

One exciting development involves leukotriene modifiers. This new class of anti-inflammatories treats mild to moderate asthma. The drug comes in chewable tablets, flavored and unflavored. Besides being easy to take, leukotriene modifiers may be more effective in reducing chronic inflammation. People who take oral anti-inflammatories will still need to use inhalers for quick relief. If tablets encourage people to take preventive medicine daily, those people may need to use inhalers less often.

Other developments include handheld nebulizers and dry-powder inhalers. Dry-powder inhalers make it easier to give correct doses of medicine. Researchers also are working on powerful new anti-inflammatories. People with asthma might need to take these medications just once a week. Someday, drugs that stop asthma altogether may be available.

Asthma and Society

Another way to reverse the rise in asthma cases involves improving the quality of life for all Americans. In particular, this means eliminating conditions that trigger asthma attacks. Everyone can get involved in efforts such as:

Establishing and maintaining indoor and outdoor air quality standards

Promoting smoke-free environments

Joining antismoking campaigns

Eliminating substandard housing

Working for adequate medical care for all people

Elton's three-year-old niece was recently diagnosed with asthma. Both Elton's sister and brother-in-law smoke. Elton wants them to quit for his niece's sake. He has shown his sister information about secondhand smoke and asthma. The information says that secondhand smoke worsens the condition of children with asthma. Elton's sister and brother-in-law are beginning to listen to him.

Elton, Age 15

Children of mothers who smoke are twice as likely to have asthma symptoms in the first five years of life. They also need hospital treatment more often than other children with asthma.

Education

Education is very important in reducing the number of asthma cases and asthma-related deaths. Both people with asthma and the public in general can learn more about this disease. People with asthma need to realize the consequences of untreated asthma. Health care providers need to teach people with asthma how to manage their illness more effectively. People everywhere need to know the symptoms of asthma. They can seek diagnosis and treatment if they have symptoms. They also can learn to be sensitive to the needs of those with asthma.

Neal had to give a report in his health class. **Neal, Age 14** He decided to talk about his asthma. Neal told the class about asthma attacks and asthma triggers. He showed them his inhaler and peak flow monitor. Neal thinks it's important that more people know about the disease. "After all," he says, "asthma affects millions of people. It even can kill them." Telling others about asthma helps Neal, too. He feels less self-conscious when he uses his inhaler at school. Students who understand about asthma no longer stare at him.

Points to Consider

What can you do to help improve the quality of life for people with asthma?

What can you do to educate other people about asthma?

How could your school help raise money for asthma research and treatment?

Glossary

allergen (AL-ur-juhn)—something that causes an allergic reaction

anti-inflammatory (an-TEE-in-FLA-muh-tor-ee)—one of the main classes of drugs used to treat asthma; anti-inflammatories reduce swelling in the lining of bronchial tubes.

bronchial tube (BRAHNG-kee-uhl TOOB)—one of the two main divisions of the trachea, or windpipe; the bronchial tubes lead into the lungs.

bronchodilator (brahng-koh-DYE-lay-tur)—one of the main classes of drugs used to treat asthma; bronchodilators relax bronchial muscles and allow the bronchial tubes to expand.

chronic (KRON-ik)—continuing for a long time; a person with a chronic disease or illness may have it throughout life.

contagious (kuhn-TAY-juhss)—capable of being spread from person to person

hormone (HOR-mohn)—a chemical that controls a body function

immune system (i-MYOON SISS-tuhm)—the system that protects the body from illness and disease; it produces cells that attack viruses and bacteria.

inflammation (in-fluh-MAY-shuhn)—redness, swelling, heat, and pain; people with asthma have inflamed airways.

mucus (MYOO-kuhss)—the clear, slippery secretion of mucous membranes; mucus moistens, cleans, and protects.

pulmonary (PUL-muh-ner-ee)—relating to the lungs

respiratory system (RESS-puh-ruh-tor-ee SISS-tuhm)—the system that allows a person to breathe; the lungs are the main organ of the respiratory system.

For More Information

Huegel, Kelly. *Young People and Chronic Illness.* Minneapolis: Free Spirit, 1998.

Silverstein, Alvin, Virginia Silverstein, and Laura Silverstein Nunn. *Asthma.* Springfield, NJ: Enslow Publishers, 1997.

Simpson, Carolyn. *Everything You Need to Know About Asthma.* New York: Rosen, 1998.

Weiss, Jonathan H. *Breathe Easy: Young People's Guide to Asthma.* New York: Magination Press, 1994.

Useful Addresses and Internet Sites

Allergy and Asthma Network/Mothers of
Asthmatics, Inc.
2751 Prosperity Avenue
Suite 150
Fairfax, VA 22031-4397
1-800-878-4403

American Academy of Allergy, Asthma
and Immunology
611 East Wells Street
Milwaukee, WI 53202-3889

Asthma and Allergy Foundation of America
1125 15th Street, NW
Suite 502
Washington, DC 20005
1-800-7-Asthma

National Asthma Education and Prevention
Program
National Heart, Lung and Blood Institute
Information Center
PO Box 30105
Bethesda, MD 20824-0105

Allergy and Asthma Network/Mothers of
Asthmatics, Inc.
http://www.aanma.org
Provides information to help families deal with
asthma and allergies

American Academy of Allergy, Asthma and
Immunology
http://www.aaaai.org
Provides information on the study and
treatment of allergic diseases

American Lung Association
http://www.lungusa.org
Offers information about fighting lung disease

Asthma and Allergy Foundation of America
http://www.aafa.org
Provides information about allergies and
asthma

Index